First published in the United Kingdom
in 2004 by:

Mansion Editions
91 Merton Mansions
Bushey Road
London sw20 8dg

+44 (0) 20 8542 7083
homer@homersykes.com
www.homersykes.com
www.mansioneditions.com

Introduction by Roger Scruton

A collector's slip case limited edition of 100
signed and numbered hardback copies of
Hunting with Hounds is available
accompanied by a signed silver gelatine
10 x 8 inch photographic print.

Original silver gelatine photographic
prints can be purchased from the author.

Concept: Homer Sykes

Design: Derek Westwood

Hardback: isbn 0-9542233-1-4
Soft back: isbn 0-9542233-2-2

Printed in Italy by EBS Verona

Hunting with Hounds

Homer Sykes

Introduction
by Roger Scruton

Published by
Mansion Editions

For Theo, Jacob and Tallulah

and all who worship at the feet of Diana and have 'Gone Hunting'

Contents

D'ye ken John Peel

D'ye ken John Peel with his coat so gay,
D'ye ken John Peel at the break of day,
D'ye ken John Peel when he's far away,
With his hounds and his horn in the morning.
For the sound of his horn brought me from my bed
And the cry of his hounds which he oft times led,
Peel's 'view hullo' would awaken the dead
Or the fox from his lair in the morning.

Yes, I ken John Peel and Ruby too,
Ranter and Ringwood and Bellman and True,
From a find to a check, from a check to a view
From a view to a death in the morning.
For the sound of his horn brought me from my bed,
And the cry of his hounds which he oft-times led,
Peel's 'view hullo' would waken the dead
Or the fox from his lair in the morning.

Then here's to John Peel from my heart and soul,
Let's drink to his health, lets finish the bowl,
We'll follow John Peel thro' fair and thro' foul
If we want a good hunt in the morning.
For the sound of his horn brought me from my bed,
And the cry of his hounds which he oft-times led,
Peel's 'view hullo' would waken the dead
Or the fox from his lair in the morning.

D'ye ken John Peel with his coat so gay,
He lived in Troutbeck once on a day,
Now he has gone far, far away,
We shall ne'er hear his voice in the morning.
For the sound of his horn brought me from my bed,
And the cry of his hounds which he oft-times led,
Peel's 'view hullo' would waken the dead
Or the fox from his lair in the morning.

John Woodcock Graves, circa 1825

Foreword

I have lived nearly all my life in the suburban sprawl of two of the greatest cities in England – as a child in a suburb of Birmingham called Northfield, and then as a young adult in Southfields, south-west London. More than a hundred years ago, both places took their names when the population of England started to move away from the countryside and great cities started to boom. Farms and fields were turned into Victorian, Edwardian, and post-world war housing estates, and the brick and concrete veneer that so threatens our countryside started to spread almost unchecked.

I love the English countryside. The sense of history that it imparts, the way it has evolved and changed to the present irregular, and apparent patchwork of fields and pastures, dotted with coverts, divided and ribboned together by rivers and streams; hedgerows, stonewalls, ancient green lanes and now alas, lifeless tarmacadam roads that lead from one village to another.

Hunting may soon enter a period of great change, and if so, it will not survive as we know it. If it is banned, then almost undoubtedly the appearance of the English country landscape will alter, as so much has been designed – all be it haphazardly – to accommodate a good day's hunting. Tens of thousands of people's lives will be affected and an historic and very English tradition will be brought to an almost abrupt halt.

Whilst working on this volume over the past year, it was quite apparent that there is a genuine anger and mystification as to why anyone with any knowledge of the countryside would want to ban hunting with hounds, and the belief that those who do want to ban it have no genuine knowledge of, or respect for, the countryside way of life. The many country people to whom I have spoken believe that legislators perceive hunting in old labour class war terms; them and us, cloth cap versus top hat – monied country toffs riding about the land in red coats shouting "tally-ho" – whereas nothing could be further from the truth.

Hunting is one of man's most natural instincts. In England, since at least the Roman times, we have hunted with hounds for both food and sport. Once the pastime of kings and those of royal birth, hunting with hounds is now a truly democratising factor in English country life. There is no top hat versus cloth cap in hunting, just the hunted, the hunters and the hounds. It is for many a livelihood, for others a way of life, and certainly a key constituent that solidifies the social fabric of country life. It is the ceremony and the sense of belonging that hunting with hounds confers, that makes the countryside in part what it is today.

Hunting with Hounds is not meant to be a comprehensive look at hunting. It reflects nine distinctly different types of hunt, where fox, deer, hare, mink, rabbit and rat are the quarry. Each of these hunts has their own visual characteristics and I hope I have been able to accentuate those differences, whilst producing a reasonably broad photographic document.

These images document hunting with hounds as it really is. The people in this book are genuine 21st century hunters, people who love their country, and want to preserve their rural way of life and a history that stretches back many hundreds of years.

There is a long tradition in Britain of hunting art. I hope that these photographs will contribute, in a 21st century way, to that body of work and the understanding of an English way of life.

Introduction
Roger Scruton

In the modern city the sense of a shared locality is being lost: people hide within their walls, public ceremonies are rare and awkward, and the old ways of celebrating neighbourhood and settlement are fast disappearing. Yet in rural communities there is one event that renews local loyalties and re-enchants the landscape, and that is hunting. Through hunting people of all occupations re-discover the moral truth that they are neighbours, and that the place where they live is the place where they are settled.

In England we witness the co-existence, as in a puzzle painting, of two visions of the landscape: that of the farmer, fiercely protecting his bounded patch, and that of the hunter, led from place to place by a quarry that recognizes neither boundaries nor laws but only the ubiquitous distinction between safety and danger. On hunting days parcelled-out farmland is suddenly transformed into the common land of the hunter-gatherer, and as suddenly lapses into its husbanded state as the hue and cry recedes. In the poetry of John Clare, in the novels of Fielding and Trollope, and in the paintings of Cotman and Crome we find striking representations of a countryside that is, as it were, doubled up, folded into two rival maps, and bearing the indelible marks of each. Nor is this doubling of the landscape witnessed only in the serious art and literature of rural England. It is equally evident in popular art and decoration. On biscuit boxes, crockery, table mats and wall prints the images of the chase are endlessly reproduced, usually dwelling on those aspects – the meet, the goodnight, the homeward-wending horsemen – that evoke the collective settlement of a common territory. The country pub establishes its credentials as a 'wayside inn' by decorating its walls with hunting prints; and the most popular song ever composed in England – 'D'ye ken John Peel?', in which the culture of hunting is lovingly surveyed and endorsed – is still sung today, long after the repertoire of folk-song has vanished from the rural consciousness.

Many of the peculiarities of English hunting are replicated in Ireland and parts of America. But nowhere outside Great Britain have they had such an effect on the landscape. Every square inch of rural England and Wales, apart from impassable or over-industrialized pockets, is situated within the boundaries of a hunt. There are some 280 hunts, each specializing in a particular quarry – deer, fox, hare or mink (the last being a recent addition, in response to the devastation caused to rivers and wildlife by the release of mink from fur farms). Although the boundaries of the hunts have been settled by negotiation, sometimes over centuries, they are a more accurate reflection of topographical, agricultural and social divisions than the county boundaries, and more eloquent by far, as a record of the landscape, its history and its meaning, than the grids, district councils and Euro-regions of the bureaucrats. Hunt boundaries are the sediments of long-lasting feelings of neighbourhood, of intense local loyalties, and of shared fortunes that have bound communities to the landscape, and made every contour into a shared possession.

Foxhounds and deerhounds hunt by scent, and this means that they will follow lines that have no relation to human visual navigation. The huntsman is there to keep them in order; but he must also follow where they lead. Following the huntsman in turn is the assembled 'field' of riders, themselves pursued by a gaggle on foot. Others string along on the country lanes, by bicycle or car. All are returning in some measure to a pre-agrarian condition. The hunter-gatherer band tracks its quarry through a landscape that belongs to both of them, since it belongs in law to neither, the chains of ownership being as yet unforged. This experience unites people in a way that is easier to observe than describe – though Hugh Brody has conveyed its force and urgency in his description of an Inuit hunting foray in *The Other Side of Eden*. And it is to this experience that we should refer for an explanation of the fervour that English hunting inspires in its followers.

The masters of hounds and their huntsmen know every field and covert in the territory over which they hunt, and are responsible for maintaining that territory in a huntable condition. Although hunting is a sport, it has also become a form of wildlife management, the purpose of which is equilibrium rather than extermination. In pursuit of this function, the hunts secure fences and boundaries for livestock, and punctuate these boundaries with jumps and gates. They maintain coverts for sanctuary, and ensure if possible that the wider habitat both supports the hunted species, and also allows its dispersal and cull. This work of stewardship is voluntary in England, paid for by the subscriptions of those who follow the hunts. And like all voluntary work, it generates social feelings and common commitments, so endorsing the hunter-gatherer sentiment that the countryside is 'ours'.

English hunting has often been celebrated as an expression of liberality. A farmer or landowner invites the hounds and followers to meet on his land. Private owners are asked if the hunt can enter, and those that agree (98%, according to recent figures) are consciously offering hospitality. However, the event also involves a collective renunciation of the usual laws of property, and a willed departure from the priorities of farming. In a sense the countryside is being 'thrown open' to its pre-historical use, and although the freedom taken by the hunt is at the same time a freedom offered by those with the power to forbid it, both parties to the deal are recapturing freedom of another and more deeply implanted kind.

In short, the hunt and its followers cross the country not by a legal right that overrides the right of property, but as though the claims of ownership have been relinquished. The hunt is re-possessing the country as a common habitat. It is re-awakening the collective sense of territory – an experience once vital to human survival, and still in some way welcomed by our genes. Plato wrote, in *The Laws*, that: 'there can be no more important kind of information than the exact knowledge of your own country; and for this as well as for more general reasons of pleasure and advantage, hunting with hounds… should be pursued by the young.' Plato's sentiments are still alive, and are expressed through the Pony Club, an institution established by the Hunts after the First World War, when it was feared that, following the loss of so many horses at the front, the equestrian culture of the English countryside might not be renewed. The purpose of the Pony Club is to initiate the young into an old sense of the landscape, as a habitat that we share with the animals. And it does this by putting the child on a pony, and awakening the hunting instinct in both of them.

It is in this context, I believe, that we should understand the peculiar excitements of hunting. The thrill of jumping is not - as many people imagine - merely an equestrian experience. It is the thrill that comes from the dissolution of a boundary, and the annihilation of all the artificial claims of title that go with it. You do this in intimate conjunction with an animal, in full and blood-warming empathy with a pack of hounds. For a brief moment you are laying aside the demands of farming, and the man-centred individualism that farming engenders, and roaming across a landscape that has not yet been 'taken into possession'. Hunting farmers maintain the sacred boundaries, precisely so as to enjoy the experience of transgressing them. Hunting is therefore one reason why England and Ireland contain the last remaining countryside in Europe with continuous walls, hedgerows and wildlife corridors between the woods and spinneys. These boundaries are very much in evidence where I live, thanks in part to the Vale of White Horse (VWH) pack of fox-hounds, whose masters manage the terrain.

Looking from my window I see the fields which it is my duty to maintain as an agricultural resource. I see rye-grass planted for silage, hedges laid to contain cattle and to keep out my neighbour's sheep, and a fenced-off corner for pigs. I worry about the docks and the thistles; I am troubled by the muck-heap and wonder whether we shall be able to spread it now that the ground is so wet. I see a gap in the hedge where the sheep could get through, and a broken culvert in the ditch which could block up in the next heavy rains. Those thoughts are the premises of husbandry, and they depend on distinguishing my rights and duties from the rights and duties of my neighbour.

But I also see a covert planted as habitat, a tiger-trap across a ditch, a hunt jump in the hedgerow and a headland set aside for horses to pass. I worry that the tiger-trap is rotten, that the hedge is now too tall to jump, that the fields are inadequately drained and are becoming impassable. Those thoughts are no longer part of husbandry, and depend on no division between 'mine' and 'thine'. I am thinking of the land as ours, the scene of a constantly renewable contest between our community of farmers and the fox with whom we come to terms by hunting him.

This sense of common ownership and common destiny is part of what turns the land into a landscape. The fields that I see from my window do not end at my boundary but stretch beyond it, to the place where the hounds of the VWH must be called off from the territory of the Old Berkshire, where 'ours' becomes 'theirs', and the riot of followers must turn at last for home.

That feeling of 'ours' is expressed in many social events besides hunting: in fun rides, farmers' breakfasts, hunt balls and point-to-points. Those events form part of an intricate web of social relations through which we join in the collective possession of our whole locality, and override our separate private claims. The 'we' feeling of the hunt is the prime reason why our boundaries are so meticulously maintained, and also so elaborately punctured. It is the cause of coverts and copses and ponds, and also the reason why many originally urban people such as myself are prepared to invest their money in a landscape that the farmers themselves can no longer maintain. The re-emergence of the hunter-gatherer sense of belonging without owning is not something recent, as our extensive and often brilliant hunting literature reveals. But, such is the heat of political passion that hunting inspires in those who have never engaged in it, that the feeling is rarely understood for what it is – a root cause of the English landscape.

13

The Blencathra Foxhounds

The Lake District is the home of six fell packs who hunt foxes on foot as the terrain is unsuitable for horses. Of these six, the Blencathra is the most famous, and sometimes referred to as the John Peel Hunt. They are based in the village of Threlkeld, nestled below the craggy scree and boulder strewn Blencathra Mountains.

John Peel is England's most famous huntsman. Born near Caldbeck in Cumbria in 1776, he eloped with Mary White when he was 20 and thanks to an inheritance from her father, Peel was able to live an independent life which he dedicated to hunting. In 1829, he was appointed huntsman to Sir Frederick Fletcher Vane. Peel is reputed to have travelled up to 60 miles a day by foot and pony in pursuit of the fox, and his fame was such that when he died in 1854 over 3,000 people attended his funeral at Caldbeck.

Originally foxes were hunted in the fells by trencher fed hounds. Each farm had a hound or two, and to protect their livelihoods like-minded farmers would meet and hunt foxes that preyed on their sheep and lambs. By about 1700, loosely formed packs of hounds were kept in kennels and hunted during the winter and then returned to their farms for the summer.

The Blencathra season starts on September 1st, the last fixture is in mid April, and from then until May 10th, the hunt are on lambing call. It's the main lambing season and any farmer who is having trouble with foxes will phone Barry Todhunter, the huntsman, for help. The following morning he will take 15 to 20 old hands, "the back bone of the pack" as he calls them, and go into the lambing field soon after dawn when there is just enough light to see. "It's completely unfamiliar territory but it's the hounds' job to strike out the scent of the fox – sometimes the fox will still be in the field, or in another near by – and they will kill it or anyway give it a real scare. It won't be back." says Todhunter. After May 10th it's the summer holiday and the hounds go out to walk, back to the same farms and cottages each year, a tradition stretching back over 300 years. They go there for the rest of their lives, and eventually retire to that particular family. About 15 to 20 hounds remain in the kennels and are looked after by the Todhunter family throughout the summer. The Blencathra are now a three-day-a-week hunt;

hunting on Tuesdays, Thursdays and Saturdays. Typically a group of 30 to 50 supporters gather at 9am for a 9.30am meet. Announcements are made as to the day's hunting, after which Barry Todhunter – who has hunted the Blencathra since 1988 – strides out after the hounds who spread and draw for a quarry's scent. Earlier that morning some followers will have made their way onto the ridges and fell tops where there is a good vantage point, to look out for a fox that is put up by the sound of the hunt in the valley below. These followers and others are in touch with the huntsman by CB radio. Once the hounds are on a line, the pace is fast and many of the supporters follow in their cars, if possible, to watch the hounds work as they stream across the mountainous terrain, others do their best to follow on foot.

Because the hounds often hunt over several valleys, and are sometimes miles ahead and out of sight, the huntsman maintains contact with the followers of the hunt by CB radio, and with the hounds by regular use of his hunting horn, calling them in when necessary. According to Barry Todhunter, "The hounds need to be able to think for themselves. For example having killed a fox on a mountain side they will find their way back to me and I will then recast them. If the fox goes to ground and can't be taken, some of the hounds will make their way back, as if to tell me to hurry up. They will take me to where the lead hounds have marked the fox."

Hunts can last for an hour and a half, and sometimes up to three hours although this is rare. The day usually finishes by 2pm depending on the weather, the time of year, and just how much work the hounds have done.

20

The Quantock Staghounds

The Quantock Hills in south-west Somerset are just sixteen miles long and six miles wide. Bordered to the south by the A358, and to the north by the A39, there are no major towns within the main group of hills, just small villages, hamlets, and scattered farms.

Crowcombe is considered by many to be the centre of the Quantocks, and The Carew Arms the centre of Crowcombe. The public bar with its well worn flagstone floor, oak settle, and open fire is adorned with hunting prints, photographs, and a mounted stag's head. The derivation of the village name is uncertain. However 'combe', in the west country relates to the Welsh 'cwm', meaning deep hollow or valley, and it has been suggested that the 'crow' comes from the Celtic and Welsh 'carw' meaning stag or deer. If so, this implies that the Quantock deer may well have been there at least as long as mankind.

The hunt is relatively new, and was founded in 1901 by Eddie Stanley of Quantock Lodge in Over Stowey, who hunted until 1907. Prior to that the Devon and Somerset Staghounds occasionally hunted the Quantocks. In 1917 the Controller of Foods at the War Cabinet asked the Master of the West Somerset Foxhounds, Sir Denis Boles, to establish a pack of staghounds to maintain the deer and provide meat.

There are now approximately 750 red deer on the hill, which is considered to be a sustainable number. However in recent years there has been a significant increase in visitors to the area which has resulted in the deer being driven down from the hill to feed on lower land that is farmed. Each deer grazes approximately three times as much as a sheep, and they also cause damage to fencing and hedges. One farmer told me there were between 20 and 30 deer in his wheat field one morning "I might have had a load of bullocks in for the damage they caused." He and many of his fellow farmers don't shoot the deer, as they are concerned about maintaining the traditional way of life in the Quantocks. "However," he continued "…poachers with their dogs certainly do shoot them. If a ban came in, there would be no more deer; they would all be shot." Depending on market conditions, a carcass can fetch from £200 to £300, and a mounted head of a stag as much as £800.

The hunting season starts in September, officially on the first Monday of the month, and goes on until the end of April. The hunt now meets only on Mondays and Thursdays as the Saturday meet has been abandoned due to the influx of tourists. During the 2003-2004 hunting season, the Quantock Staghounds culled twelve autumn stags and 45 hinds; a further 13 spring stags were taken between March and April. The hunt gets called out to about 40 casualties a year – these are either road accidents involving deer, or cases where poachers have shot and wounded their quarry, later to abandon it. It is the huntsman's job to dispatch these distressed animals.

On an average day there may be 80 mounted followers, and up to 100 foot followers in vehicles who gather at the meet, usually for an 11am start. From early morning a harbourer will have been out and tracked a suitable stag for culling. (One that has passed its prime or is going back, i.e. the number of points on its antlers is decreasing.) The information as to its whereabouts is passed back to the huntsman and masters at the meet. The hunt then moves off to a location near where the stag has been seen. The huntsman takes five and a half couple of the most experienced hounds known as tufters and on horseback, or sometimes on foot, will draw the area searching for the quarry. When it has been located, the stag rises, and the hounds take the line. The hunt usually lasts for three to four hours but on occasion it can go on well into the early evening.

The quarry is eventually exhausted and stands at bay surrounded by the hounds, who never touch it. A specially trained member of the hunt, known as the gun carrier, will dispatch the deer at close range to ensure that it does not escape injured. It will then be disembowelled; the hounds eat the entrails. Sometimes a young hunter is blooded, an initiation process where the blood of the stag is smeared on the face. The carcass is then taken back to the kennels to be hung and eventually distributed to those farmers whose land the hunt has passed over, and whose crops the stag had been feeding off.

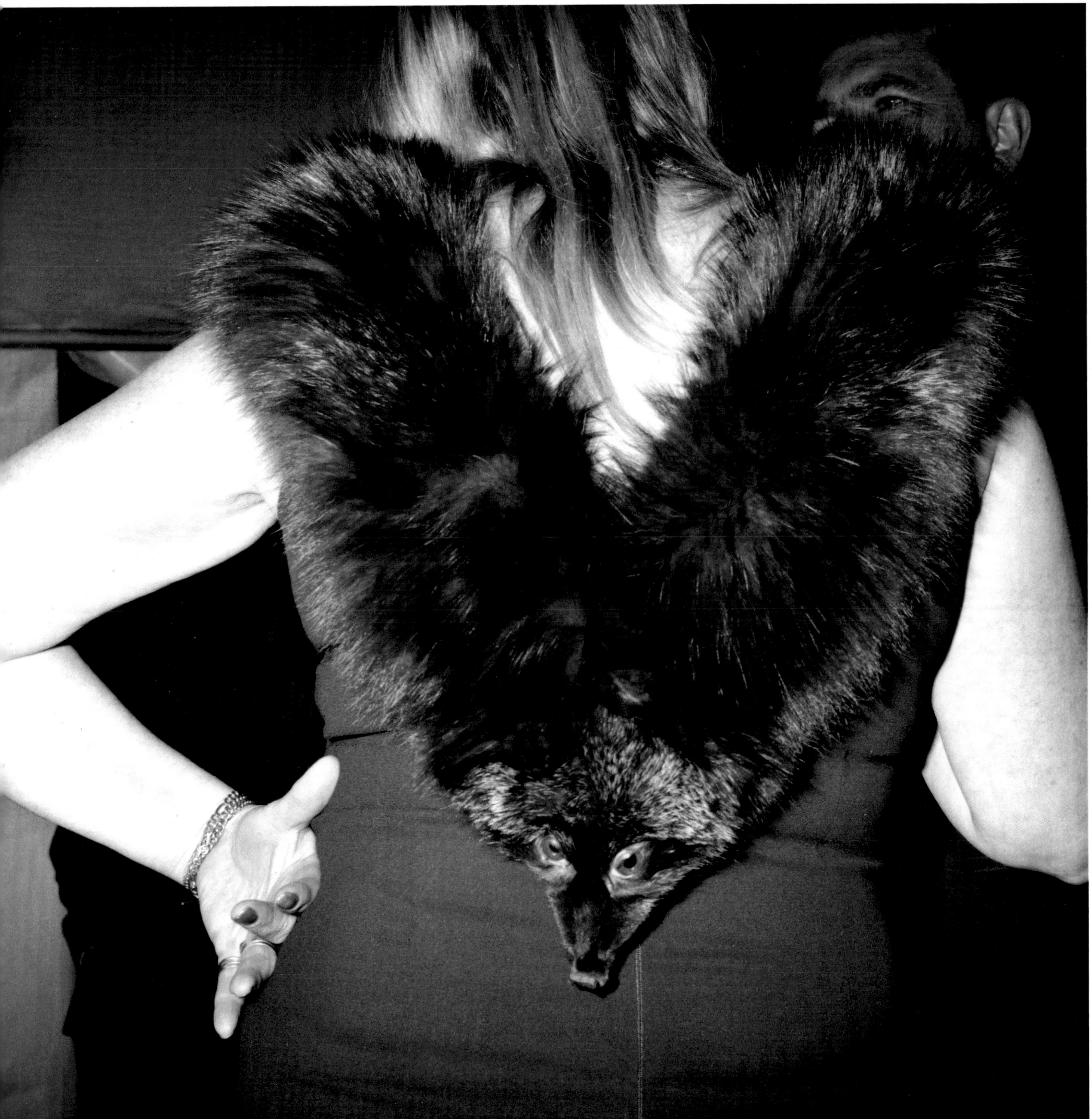

43

The Dummer Beagles

The Romans brought over small Greek hounds for hunting and trading, and the Saxons are known to have hunted hare, and were exempt from the Forest Laws drawn up by King Canute in 1016.

The hunting of the hare with packs of hounds kept by the aristocracy and the landed gentry only started to decline during the 19th century, when foxhunting became the premier English field sport.

Today there are 100 recognised packs of beagles, bassets and harriers. In 1891 the Association of Masters of Harriers and Beagles was founded, and it is still the governing body of hare hunting in Britain. There are approximately 70 beagle packs in England, 20 of which are hunted professionally.

Probably the finest beagle pack in England is the Dummer, who take their name from the Hampshire village. They were originally a private pack, owned and bred by Sir Newton Ryecroft, who moved his country-seat in 1939 from Dummer to Little Rissington, Gloucestershire, which is where they are still kennelled. During the summer several litters of puppies are bred. They go out to walk at about eight weeks old to farms and homes of supporters where they learn their names and basic discipline. They appear at the puppy show usually held in June the following year as new entry, and start hunting at the beginning of the new season.

The season starts after the summer harvest is brought in, generally in early September. This period is called autumn hunting, and it is when the young beagles are taught to hunt. According to Senior Master, Robin Leach, "Given half a chance they will hunt anything that moves, like a pheasant or rabbit, and that habit has to be stopped. They are like children, some learn more quickly than others, and all follow the example set by the more experienced beagles that they hunt with, and learn from." The Dummer opening meet is held during the second week of October, with the season ending in mid March.

The Dummer are a two-day-a-week bitch only pack, hunting on Wednesdays and Saturdays.

About 20 regulars turn out on Wednesdays, and at the weekend as many as 50 followers may attend the meet - regardless of the weather. Typically the followers gather at the meet at 12 o'clock and a cap is collected, four pounds for members, and seven pounds for non-members. Robin Leach makes the day's announcements and the huntsman and the whips will then move off to draw. The beagles will be encouraged to spread out to find a hare. On Saturdays there are as many as four or five whips positioned out on the flanks, whose job it is to keep an eye out for a hare, and then pass that information back to the huntsman. Two further mobile whips, in cars, monitor the road traffic situation.

Hounds are counted in couples, and the Dummer hunt with 18½. Once they have a line, the beagles will speak or give tongue as they follow the scent, with the huntsman running with them. As many as 25 miles or more can be covered in a day, hunting several different hares. Hares are territorial, and when they are put up by the hounds they often run roughly in a circle. The hare may be referred to as going left handed, or right handed. Sometimes a hare takes off in a straight line, and is then called a travelling jack. These hares are thought to have been out of their territory looking for a mate. On average, the Dummer account for about one hare a day. Hunting usually goes on until the late afternoon, though on occasion they have been known to hunt by moonlight!

The less athletic hunt followers view the proceedings from high ground or a hill where it is quite easy to watch the hounds at work, following the line of the hare. For the more agile followers, the day can be spent clambering over stone walls, scrabbling through hedges, jumping ditches, or if the hare is coming towards you, lying very still on the ground and pointing with sticks, or waving a white handkerchief. To indicate that they have seen the hunted hare they holloa – but no more than three times.

48

54

The Valley Minkhounds

In 1975 otter hunting was banned in England and Wales on conservation grounds, and many of these hunts switched their attention to the hunting of mink. Mink are not native to Britain, and in the 1920s, North American mink were introduced and bred on fur farms. The wild mink are the result of releases or escapes and are a self-sustaining feral population.

They are extremely elusive, and notoriously difficult to trap. The damage they cause to the natural environment is substantial. They are opportunistic feeders, and eat a variety of mammals, including hares, rabbits, hedgehogs, as well as nesting birds, and fish. Mink are considered to be one of main causes for the decline in the numbers of water vole, and many countrymen and river keepers tell of the disappearance of moorhens, kingfishers, and ducks as soon as mink appear in their area. The Valley Minkhounds usually catch about two-thirds of all the mink they find, as they are able to track them in water and on the land. But hunting them with hounds also assists with other forms of pest control by pin pointing where they are living, so that both game and river keepers can then lay traps.

The Masters of Minkhounds' Association was formed in 1978 and now represents 24 mink hunts in England and Wales, a few of which are privately owned. The majority are subscription packs such as the Valley Minkhounds, which was started in 1990 by Aidan Slatter along with half a dozen fellow enthusiasts. The Valley Minkhounds have eleven couple of hounds in kennels and always hunt with as many as are fit. Other hunts may go out with fewer hounds, but Aidan Slatter believes that, "they learn nothing sitting in the kennels, and so they might as well go hunting." Their pack of hounds is a combination of otterhounds, foxhounds and cross breeds; they have recently initiated a small breeding programme.

The Valley Minkhounds meet each Saturday, usually about midday, at a pre-arranged location, and hunt a particular stretch of the rivers Kennet or Enborne until the late afternoon. They occasionally join forces with other hunts, and this swells the number of followers from about a handful, to over 20. Every one attending pays a cap of £5, though there is also a family subscription of £40 per annum. Aidan Slatter, who hunts the hounds, and his two whips set off at a cracking rate, the supporters following at a much more leisurely pace. "Ninety percent of the day is spent walking along the river bank and waiting for the hounds to mark," according to a regular hunt supporter. For others, it's simply a day out in the country, and a "chance to go somewhere you would not normally get to."

The hounds will draw a riverbank, one hound will speak and the others will then usually pile in, creating an almighty chorus as they mark a spot where the quarry's scent is strongest. Occasionally, if a mink is discovered, it will be killed quickly by the hounds. However, the river banks of the Kennet and Enborne are very lush and overgrown, and there is a pretty good chance that the mink will slip off out of sight, up a tree, into a drainage culvert, or simply swim underwater across the river and away. In a good year they will cull about 50 mink.

64

66

Hare Coursing

Coursing is one of the world's oldest field sports, dating back at least to the time of the Pharaohs, and it was probably introduced to Britain by the Romans, along with the common brown hare.

The object of coursing under National Coursing Club rules is to test these "gazehounds" who chase exclusively by sight, unlike fox and staghounds, who hunt by scent. The first coursing club in England was founded in Swaffham, Norfolk in 1776, and still thrives. During the 1800s with the advent of rail travel, coursing became very popular. Huge crowds attended the principal meetings at Altcar, Ashdown Park, and Stonehenge. The Waterloo Cup, the classic event of the coursing season, has been run at Altcar near Liverpool since 1836. William Lynn, owner of the old Waterloo Hotel in Liverpool, originally ran the coursing meet in tandem with his steeplechase at nearby Aintree, which the local press dubbed "The Grand National". By the late 1800s the Waterloo Cup was a major national event. Huge daily crowds were common, carrier pigeons carried the results to all major cities, and in London the Stock Exchange closed early when news of the winners arrived. With the advent of the 20th century, the popularity of coursing gradually began to decline. By 1926 entrepreneurs were building greyhound-racing tracks on the outskirts of our great cities, electric hares had become a possibility, and with the advent of electric light, the working class audience that coursing had always attracted were able to go to the dog track after a day's work.

The rules laid down in Swaffham in 1776 are almost exactly the same as those that they course by today. It is the agility of the greyhound, its speed, stamina and its ability to turn a hare that counts. If a dog kills a hare, it does not necessarily win the course. National Coursing Club rules that are applied today do not permit coursing between March 1st and September 30th, so that the hares remain undisturbed during the main part of the breeding season, although in practice there is not much coursing until mid October.

Meets usually start in mid-morning, the beaters having been out much earlier. It is their job to drive the hares from adjoining fields, one by one, onto the running ground. Only two hounds course at a time, and each wears a distinguishing red or white collar. Once the hare is on the running field, the slipper, in his traditional hunting pink jacket, releases the hounds simultaneously from their holding leashes, but only after the hare has been seen to be fit, and has been given a sporting 100 yard law.

A judge on horseback follows the course, and awards points to either the red or white collar: up to three points for the lead up, one point for a full turn, and a half point for a wrench. Points are also deducted. No points are awarded for a kill. Coursing stakes are simple knockout competitions, and the winners of each round progress through the competition until two hounds remain to contest the final stake.

An average course lasts less than a minute. Hares have greater stamina than greyhounds, and the initial speed advantage of the dogs is soon overcome. A hare weighing 7 to 9 lbs can turn in its own length, while a greyhound weighing six or seven times as much will invariably overshoot. As the hounds only chase by sight, they stop when the hare has escaped out of their sight. This is the end of the course. In the 2003-2004 coursing season 126 hares were killed, an average of one hare killed in every ten courses.

When a hare is brought down, death is usually instantaneous; the rules insist on four pickers-up, strategically placed on the coursing ground, to ensure that a hare brought down is quickly and humanely dispatched.

72

74

Rat, Rabbiting and Lurcherwork

The Royal Albert Ratting Club was founded in 1997 by a group of friends, in response to the proposed government bill of that time, which would have outlawed the hunting of rats and other quarry species with dogs.

Peter Beech chairman and founder member says, "…they (the government in London) took our work off us, and now they want our pleasure too." He believed that by forming a society their position within the wider hunting community would be strengthened and that they would, "…look better, and would not be so susceptible to being picked off by 'antis'." The seven members gather on the first Wednesday of each month at The Royal Albert Hotel, Blacker Hill, Barnsley to discuss club-hunting business and to have a few pints.

They meet each Sunday morning at 8am near junction 36 of the M1 motorway with their dogs – Meg, Sandy, Lady, Timber, Buck, Jess, Paddy, and Gill, and head off to a pre-arranged local farm where they hunt for a couple of hours, often killing up to 25 or more rats.

Since appearing on Yorkshire television in 2003, they have become well known in their community. It is not uncommon for farmers to call them up and ask them to come around rather than pay £25 for a registered pest control officer, who as Peter says, only puts poison down, which the rats become immune to in time. There is no secondary killing with dogs, whereas there is with poison.

The International Fund for Animal Welfare estimates that there are 200,000 lurcher owners in Great Britain, of which approximately 120-150,000 are working lurchers, ranging from the enthusiast who puts his dog on a rabbit for the pot while out walking, to lurchermen who take their sport more seriously and go out lamping, netting or taking part in hare coursing stakes and for pest control. The coursing season starts on September 15th and ends on March 10th. Pest control undertaken by lurchermen at the request of a landowner or farmer can take place all year, however due care is given to the quarry's breeding season.

Rural myth has it that the lurcher is the dog of the poacher, it once may have been but those times have long since passed. Today the vast majority of lurcher owners are law abiding hunting enthusiasts who enjoy nothing better than seeing their dogs work or watching them lie by a fire in the comfort of their own homes. A family pet and silent hunting dog, the lurcher does not draw attention to itself by barking. It is not a breed of dog but a type, produced by mating the greyhound (sometimes a whippet or saluki) to another working dog, often a border collie, to suit the specific needs of the lurcher owner.

Lurchermen who choose to hunt rabbits during the day often enlist the help of a ferret to chase rabbits from their warren once their lurcher has marked it, while those who run their dogs at night to rabbit, hare and fox, use a powerful lamp. This practice is known as lamping, and is a most efficient way of hunting nocturnal quarry species that feed during the hours of total darkness. A high powered lamp is used to illuminate the quarry. Once caught in the beam, a rabbit will squat and remain frozen, the lurcherman works his way forward towards the rabbit and as it moves, he slips his dog, illuminating the rabbit as it runs off with the lurcher in pursuit.

Alan Tyer runs The Old English and Colonial Lurcher Club, and believes that single-handed hare coursing is the purest and fairest form of hunting. One dog against one hare, the hare always being given at least a 100 yard law. Only the fittest hares survive and the gene pool is kept strong. Typically ten lurchermen will spread out in a line across a field where it is known there are hare. Walking slowly in a straight line a lurcher will be slipped on a hare that is put up in front of it. The Old English and Colonial Lurcher Club will hunt a particular piece of land four or five times a year taking roughly 100 hares off it in a season. This negates the need for the farmer to have a hare shoot where killing is completely indiscriminate, often wiping out the entire hare population. They hunt under a strict code of practice laid down by the Association of Lurcher Clubs that was formed in 1995 and which is a member of the Council of Hunting.

The Duke of Beaufort's Hunt

Foxhunting in England is comparatively recent compared to the hunting of stag and hare. By the late 13th century King Edward I had a royal pack of foxhounds but it was not until several centuries later that foxhunting became more popular, and took the form that we know today. There are now 181 foxhunting packs registered with the Master of the Foxhounds' Association. Perhaps one of the oldest is the Duke of Beaufort's Hunt which is based at the Badminton estate in Gloucestershire, home of the Duke of Beaufort, whose predecessor the 10th Duke, was known in the world of hunting simply as "Master".

For the cognoscenti, Badminton is the capital of the foxhunt in England. The earliest records of hounds being kennelled at Badminton date back to 1640, when the then Marquis of Worcester mainly hunted deer as well as hare and fox. However it was not until 1762 that the young 5th Duke of Beaufort, returning with his staghounds after a dull day's sport, put them into Silk Wood, and had such a fine run with a fox, that thereafter he concentrated exclusively on foxhunting.

Depending on farming conditions, the hunting season starts towards the middle of August, this is known as autumn hunting for which subscribers and farmers wear rat-catcher. When the season proper starts, which for most hunts – including the Beaufort – is usually on the first Saturday in November, their attire changes to their blue and buff coats, and occasionally for the men, silk top hats, while the farmers wear their black coats and hunt buttons. Very rarely these days, a lady might still ride side-saddle wearing a riding habit and veil. Rat-catcher is worn again for the last month of the season in spring and after the point-to-point races, when the hunt by tradition goes into its hill country.

The Beaufort hunts four days a week – Monday, Wednesday, Thursday, and Saturday and in the autumn they often hunt on many Tuesdays, averaging 125 hunting days a year. On Saturdays, the Beaufort hunts the country around the park and the villages near Badminton. In all the Beaufort country covers 760 square miles, though in recent times this has been reduced by 260 acres due to the advance of urbanisation. Not all hunts are as large as the Beaufort, who have over 250 mounted subscribers and over 100 mounted farmers or members of their families.

Typically on a Saturday, as many as 200 mounted riders and perhaps up to 150 to 200 foot and car followers gather together at 10.45am for the meet. Sometimes a traditional warming stirrup cup is served, following which the master, hunt staff and hounds will move off to the area where it is planned to commence hunting. Many hours of planning will have gone in to each hunting day. The mounted field will follow at a distance, and the foot followers in their vehicles will drive off to suitable vantage-points. The hounds will be encouraged to spread out to draw for a fox in woodland or rough ground. If they scent a fox, the hounds will speak. If the fox is still in the vicinity he will leave as quickly and quietly as possible, and if seen by those on point they will holloa, or call gone away, to let the huntsman know that he has gone. The huntsman then urges on the hounds to pick up the scent again, and using their incredible scenting ability, the hounds will hunt the fox until they catch it - or lose it or it goes to ground. Huntsmen say that hunting is the most humane method of fox control because it is entirely natural and selective, as a hunted fox is either caught and killed instantaneously or gets away.

The length of the chase may vary considerably from a few minutes to well over an hour or even longer, but the average is about 15 to 20 minutes. It is rare for any followers to be present at the kill. Quite frequently, instead of being caught by the hounds, the fox will go to ground, typically in a fox earth. Once the fox has gone to ground, and at the request of the landowner, the fox can be bolted from the earth and shot at close range by experienced and licensed terrier men working under the strict rules of the Masters of the Foxhounds' Association.

94

103

Captions

PAGE 9
The Blencathra foxhounds. Near Braithwaite, Cumbria.

PAGE 11
Spectators take cover at Greyhound 2000. Near Six Mile Bottom, Newmarket, Suffolk.

The Blencathra Foxhounds

PAGE 15
Hounds develop a strong bond with the families they go out to walk with each summer. The meet at the Old Crown. Hesket Newmarket, Cumbria.

PAGE 16
Barry Todhunter manages the hounds outside The Old Crown while many supporters meet inside to sample the locally brewed beers: Helvellyn Gold, Skiddaw Special Bitter, Blencathra Bitter, Old Carrocks Strong Ale, or perhaps, Doris' 90th Birthday Ale. Hesket Newmarket, Cumbria.

PAGE 17
Dick Peel collects the cap. Dick usually collects around £120 in cap money, which goes towards the upkeep of the hounds. Hesket Newmarket, Cumbria.

PAGE 18 & PAGE 19
Coffee, cake and biscuits are provided by Mrs Dorothy Roper in her kitchen. Hall Garth Farm, Near Braithwaite, Cumbria.

PAGE 21
Barry Todhunter, the huntsman, gathers up the hounds before recasting. His two working terriers always accompany him. He celebrated 30 years with the Blencathra Foxhounds in 2004, first as whip and then as huntsman, and is only the seventh huntsman since 1862. Near Braithwaite, Cumbria.
The Blencathra foxhounds are directly descended from John Peel's original pack. Two years after John Peel died, the pack of hounds was dispersed and Peel's best and favourite hound 'Briton' and his couple companion, a bitch named 'Cruel', were bought by Squire Crozier who also bought a second couple of hounds. These hounds of Peel's were mated with

the best of Mr Crozier's, and used extensively for stud purposes – justifying to some extent the description of the Blencathra as 'Peel's old pack'. After 30 years Squire Crozier felt that the time had arrived for his pack to be turned into a subscription hunt, and at a meeting in Threlkeld on January 21st 1870, the Blencathra was formed in its present state.

PAGE 22 & PAGE 23
Hunt supporters follow the hounds from their vehicles as they stream across the mountainous terrain. Near Braithwaite, Cumbria.

PAGE 25
The Blencathra foxhounds are considered by many to be one of the fastest packs in the country. They hunt a mixed pack of dogs and bitches, 45 are kennelled. If the hunt is in the valleys and away from the roads 35-40 hounds go out to hunt, but if they are hunting near Keswick or main roads, then only 20 or so will hunt those days. Near Braithwaite, Cumbria.
The Blencathra hunt some of the most spectacular country in Britain, which extends from Caldbeck in the north to the summits of Helvellyn, Dunmail Raise, Steel Fell and High Raise. Their country continues through Angle Tarn and Esk Hause to Scafell Pike, Great Gable and the top of Honister Pass. From there the boundary goes over Dale Head, Robinson, Newlands Hause, Eel Crag and Grisedale Pike, crossing Bassenthwaite Lake to Scarness, Orthwaite, Uldale and back to Caldbeck.

PAGE 27
A fox has gone to earth, Barry Todhunter blocks the earth before calling off the hounds prior to the arrival of the terrier men. During the 2003-2004 season approximately 100 foxes were accounted for. Near Braithwaite, Cumbria.

PAGE 28
A hound finds its way back to the pack. Near Braithwaite, Cumbria.

PAGE 29
Barry Todhunter calls in missing hounds at the end of the day's hunt. Near Braithwaite, Cumbria.

The Quantock Staghounds

PAGE 31
A mounted stag's head looks down on the revellers who have spilled out of the hunt ball marquee and into Bagborough House. Bagborough, Somerset.

PAGE 32 *left and right*
Tickets are keenly sort after for the hunt ball, which is a high point in the social calendar. The huge marquee set up on the lawn houses a lively party that continues on into the small hours. Bagborough House, Bagborough, Somerset.

PAGE 33
A stole is worn nonchalantly at the hunt ball. Bagborough House, Bagborough, Somerset.

PAGE 34
The horse box is used to house the refreshments provided for the hunt and hunt followers. Woodlands, Holeford, Somerset.

PAGE 35
The whipper-in and the huntsman keep the hounds gathered together and separated from the main body of the hunt and their guests. Woodlands, Holeford, Somerset.

PAGE 36 & PAGE 37
A great deal of time is spent waiting while the huntsman tries to locate the quarry's scent. Quantock Hills, Somerset.

PAGE 38
A loyal body of supporters, many of whom once used to be mounted followers, follow the hunt in their cars. Quantock Hills, Somerset.

PAGE 39
Richard Downs, the huntsman, leads the mounted field. Quantock Hills, Somerset.

PAGE 40
Loyal hunt followers can be rewarded with the hooves of the stag. Quantock Hills, Somerset.

PAGE 41
The stag is gutted and its entrails fed to the hounds before it is taken back to the kennels to be hung, and later distributed to local farmers. Quantock Hills, Somerset.

PAGE 43
The Quantock Staghounds' Antler Competition is an integral part of the August Bank Holiday Monday Quantock Show. These antlers are ones that have been found by enthusiastic antler collectors, and all have been shed naturally. Prizes are awarded for a variety of classes, ranging from Best Autumn Pair to Spring Best Single and Champion of Champions.

The Dummer Beagles

PAGE 45
Steven Duckmanton, huntsman, and the only fulltime member of staff. The Dummer traditionally hunt a bitch only pack, as they are considered faster and more biddable. Manor Farm, Upper Slaughter, Gloucestershire.

PAGE 46
Each Saturday there is a well supported raffle for a bottle of whisky, the profits helping to offset some of the costs of running the Dummer Beagles. Manor Farm, Upper Slaughter, Gloucestershire.

PAGE 47
A lawn meet at Manor Farm, Icomb, Gloucestershire. It's a very social occasion with the host providing ample refreshment.

PAGE 49
Neville Barton offers Susie Storey a helping hand. Manor Farm, Upper Slaughter, Gloucestershire.

PAGE 50 *left*
Rosie, Lady Northampton indicates the direction of the hare. Manor Farm, Upper Slaughter, Gloucestershire.

PAGE 50 *right*
A high vantage-point provides a better view of the field. Manor Farm, Upper Slaughter, Gloucestershire.

PAGE 51 *left and right*
The hare is territorial and often runs in a rough circle. A well known and true saying with the hare hunting fraternity is "The first shall be last, and the last first". Court Hayes Farm, Wyck Beacon, Gloucestershire.

PAGE 52
The Dummer hunt with permission of the Master of the Fox Hounds' Association. Their country takes in the Heythrope, Warwick and the Cotswold foxhunting country. Manor Farm, Icomb, Gloucestershire.

PAGE 53
At the end of the day, very exhausted and thirsty beagles drink from a cattle trough. Manor Farm, Upper Slaughter, Gloucestershire.
In the 14th century, Chaucer referred to them in the Canterbury Tales as "smale houndes". In Tudor times, Queen Elizabeth I had her own pack of "Singing Beagles" and King James I affectionately referred to his wife as his "Dear little Beagle".

PAGE 55
Steven Duckmanton with hunting horn and whip. It's unusual, but up to two and a half brace of hares have been culled in a day. Manor Farm, Upper Slaughter, Gloucestershire.

The Valley Minkhounds

PAGE 57
Mink are very elusive, they climb trees and swim rivers, and often manage to slip quietly away when spotted. Near Aldermaston, Berkshire.

PAGE 58
Aidan Slatter takes the hounds across a fast flowing part of the river Kennet. Near Aldermaston, Berkshire.

PAGE 59 *left*
Joey the terrier man rescues one of his four Patterdale terriers that had become tangled up in brambles and overhanging undergrowth on the river Kennet. Near Aldermaston, Berkshire.

PAGE 59 *right*
A mink is spotted high up a tree eating a duck. The terrier man gets a helping hand, and climbs the tree to force the quarry down. When it came down, it somehow managed to slip away into the thick riverbank undergrowth. Near Aldermaston, Berkshire.

PAGE 60
Followers resting on the river bank on a very warm summer's day. Near Aldermaston, Berkshire.

PAGE 61
The quarry has escaped into a broken culvert. River Enborne, near Aldermaston, Berkshire.

PAGE 62
Perry Stares, Master of the Hampshire Minkhounds, on the river Enborne at a joint meet with the Valley Minkhounds. Near Aldermaston, Berkshire.

PAGE 63
Tom Dover, a regular follower, listens for a mink that may have escaped down a rotten tree trunk, and into the root system. Near Aldermaston, Berkshire.

PAGE 65
Aidan Slatter, huntsman, with his two whips, Michael Riching and Simon Haines, and some of their hounds. Near Aldermaston, Berkshire.

PAGE 66
Whipper-in, Simon Haines, swims across the river Kennet following the hounds who are in pursuit of their quarry. Near Aldermaston, Berkshire.

PAGE 67
Whipper-in, Michael Riching, carries a hound back to the wagon in the traditional manner. Near Aldermaston, Berkshire.

Hare Coursing

PAGE 69
Slipper, Wayne Drew, with two greyhounds wearing identifying red and white collars. He is looking over the hedge towards a group of beaters who are driving hares, one at a time, towards the coursing field. The Cotswold Coursing Club Meet, near Kilkenny, Gloucestershire.

PAGE 70 *left*
A hunting family sit out the rain in their car. The bonnet is adorned with a mascot of a common brown hare in full flight. Greyhound 2000 Meet. Near Six Mile Bottom, Newmarket, Suffolk.

PAGE 70 *right*
Geoff Fuller, a spectator at the Waterloo Cup, leans on a walking stick carved with the head of a greyhound holding a hare in its mouth, made by fellow enthusiast Paul Wayman. Near Altcar, Lancashire.

PAGE 71
Two owners with their greyhounds wait for a signal to walk their hounds down to the starting position during the Greyhound 2000 Meet. Near Six Mile Bottom, Newmarket, Suffolk.

PAGE 72
A liquid lunch is enjoyed in the members' enclosure at the Waterloo Cup. The Waterloo Cup is considered the blue riband, or Ascot, of the hare coursing season. Near Altcar, Lancashire.

PAGE 73
Spectators at the Waterloo Cup relax between courses. The running field is in front of them. On all formal coursing grounds there are a series of floughs incorporated into the design of the field. Near Altcar, Lancashire.

PAGE 75
The Waterloo Cup, a three-day event, has been run near Altcar since 1836. In 1874, 80,000 spectators turned out. In 2004, a very respectable 10,000 people attend including a large contingent from Ireland and a smaller number of enthusiasts from mainland Europe and America.

PAGE 76 & PAGE 77
On a bitterly cold February day members of the Swaffham Coursing Club meet near Narborough, Norfolk. The judge on horseback monitors each course. He carries with him a small red and white flag, which he waves to indicate to the flagman which greyhound has won. The flagman then flies the appropriate coloured flag.

PAGE 78
Family groups gather for a day's coursing at the Waterloo Cup. Near Altcar, Lancashire.

PAGE 79
Lepus europaeus, or the common brown hare, is larger and more athletic than its cousin, the rabbit. Near Narborough, Norfolk.

PAGE 80
Stephen Little, a well known bookmaker, wears a fur coat at the Waterloo Cup. Near Altcar, Lancashire.

PAGE 81
A trainer rubs down one of his greyhounds at the end of the Waterloo Cup. Near Altcar, Lancashire.

Rat, Rabbiting and Lurcherwork

PAGE 83
"Rattus Norvegicus Originall caught at Carr House Farm, Howsbrook, Barnsley, Yorkshire by Meg, Sandy, and others in June 2001." It measured 20.5 inches long and weighed 1lb 7oz, and is now displayed in the home of club member Brian Oliver. Barnsley, Yorkshire.

PAGE 84
Sunday morning digging out rats. Hunshell Farm, Greenmoor, Barnsley, Yorkshire.
The membership subscription costs £5 a month, which goes towards club activities. Last year they attended a Game Fair, the Countryside Alliance march in London, and went on various rabbiting expeditions on the Yorkshire moors.

PAGE 85
A farm rat, it is estimated that one rat costs a farmer 50p a week in grain and damage. Bromley Farm, Bramley, Barnsley, Yorkshire.
It is estimated that there are over 60 million rats in England, and they are on the increase. Wherever you are in an urban environment you are never more than 15 feet away from one.

PAGE 86
Rabbits fresh for the pot. *The Three Stags Head* specialises in real ale and fresh game, when available. Wardlow, Derbyshire.

PAGE 87
Paul and Lee Wayman out lamping with Paul's lurcher Bittern. Lee carries an air rifle. Near junction 18 of the M1, Warwickshire.
Paul is a typical lurcherman who has been hunting rabbits since a child, first with ferrets, then with whippets, and now with a lurcher, and describes them as "having so much stamina, all the best breeds mingled together to make the ultimate hunting machine." He usually manages to go out lamping two or three nights a week. The best night he has ever had was when "the father of my present dog caught and retrieved 23 rabbits in one three hour session." More often than not, he will take home about ten rabbits after a night out lamping. As with ratting, there is an element of pest control, his job is to keep the rabbits down for the farmer whose land he has permission to hunt over, but it's the pleasure he gets in seeing his dog Bittern (a Bedlington terrier, whippet, collie, greyhound second cross) work, that keeps him out hunting in the middle of the night.

PAGE 89
John Armstrong from the North East Lurcher Club, a guest of The Old English and Colonial Lurcher Club hunting in Lincolnshire on a cold and blustery February day. Barbara Tyer wraps up to keep the wind and rain out.

The Duke of Beaufort's Hunt

PAGE 91
The traditional Boxing Day Meet is held at Worcester Lodge, on the Badminton estate. It is usual for several hundred mounted followers and an equal number of foot followers to attend along with a TV crew or two, as well as a number of freelance photographers. Near Didmarton, Gloucestershire 2002.

PAGE 92
Foot followers discuss the coming day's hunting. Easton Grey House, Easton Grey, Wiltshire.

PAGE 93
The meet at Easton Grey House. Easton Grey, Wiltshire.
It was at Easton Grey that the former Prince of Wales planted an oak tree to commemorate the time he spent there enjoying the 1922-1923 hunting season. The present Prince, the Princes, and their family friends still hunt with the Beaufort.

PAGE 94
A grandmother and her granddaughter. Upton Grove House, near Avening, Gloucestershire.

PAGE 95
A young rider on an unusual furry horse. The Boxing Day Meet, Worcester Lodge, near Didmarton, Gloucestershire 2002.
Hunting makes a huge contribution to the local rural economy. It is estimated that around 800 horses are kept in the Beaufort country for the purpose of hunting.

PAGE 97
The mounted field wait in a clearing on the Badminton estate, while the huntsman and hounds draw a covert. The Boxing Day Meet, Worcester Lodge, near Didmarton, Gloucestershire 2002. Unlike most hunts, the huntsman and whips do not wear traditional red coats, they wear green which was the colour of the livery worn by outdoor servants – coachmen and hunt servants. The Heythrop Hunt's livery is identical, echoing the days when all that country was hunted by the same pack.

PAGE 99
Silk top hats are still worn by some hunt subscribers, who traditionally wear blue coats with buff facings, and are known as the Blue and Buff. This fashion can be traced back to the family's Plantaganet forebear John of Gaunt, Duke of Lancaster, whose colours were azure and gold. The Boxing Day Meet, Worcester Lodge near Didmarton, Gloucestershire 2002.

PAGE 100
The hunt in full gallop across the countryside in pouring rain. Near Luckington, Gloucestershire.

PAGE 101
A mounted follower takes a jump in pouring rain. Near Luckington, Gloucestershire.

PAGE 102
The meet at the home of Mrs Elizabeth Pope to celebrate her 90th birthday. A chocolate cake in the form of a mounted fox's mask is presented, before being distributed amongst the well wishers. Near Avening, Gloucestershire.

PAGE 103
The Beaufort hunt 15½ couple of hounds, though 60 couple are kept in kennels. Luckington, Gloucestershire.

PAGE 104
The puppy show at Badminton House, Badminton, Gloucestershire.
Bred for their nose, stamina and character, these hounds win numerous competitions. The earliest records of hounds being kennelled at Badminton date back to 1640. Ian Farquhar, the present Joint Master, who has hunted the hounds since 1985, says that they are probably the most chronicled animals kept by man.

PAGE 105
The puppy show at Badminton House. It is the highlight of the summer season, where puppy walkers can proudly watch their charges do their best. Badminton, Gloucestershire.

All the photographs in Hunting with Hounds *were taken in* 2003-2004 *unless otherwise stated.*

Acknowledgements

I would particularly like to thank Beth Bluck who helped me rethink some of the text and who took much time and trouble copy editing. Her good advice and her continuous support throughout the project is greatly appreciated. Chris Austin, Director of the Association of Masters of Harriers and Beagles, who put me in touch with the Dummer Beagles, and kindly checked my text on the Dummer Beagles and the Hare Coursing section for factual accuracy. Jo Aldridge who helped me with facts about the Duke of Beaufort's Hunt, made suggestions and checked it for accuracy. Elizabeth Walton who first took me hare coursing and sparked my interest in *Hunting with Hounds*. Geoff Howard for his sound advice and good council. Glen Brent for the time and trouble he took to make the beautiful prints for this book and my previous book *On the Road Again*. Ken Sethi of Genesis Digital Imaging for his support. Derek Westwood for once again working on the design.

The Dummer Beagles
Robin Leach, Joint Master of the Dummer Beagles.
Robert Smith, Joint Master of the Dummer Beagles.
Margot Wiffin, Joint Master of the Dummer Beagles.
Steven Duckmanton, Huntsman.
Robert Parks, Whipper-in.
Diana Woolley, Hunt Club Secretary.
Rosie, Lady Northampton.
Stephen Parker.
Susie Storey.
Neville Barton.

The Quantock Staghounds
Enid Baker, Joint Master of the Quantock Staghounds.
Brian Palmer, Joint Master of the Quantock Staghounds.
Max A'Brook, Joint Master of the Quantock Staghounds.
Philip and Diana Brooke-Popham.
Richard Downs, Huntsman.
Edward Chown, Whipper-in.
Richard Coates, Hunt Club Secretary.
Derek Hicks.
David Houghton.

The Blencathra Foxhounds
Doctor Jim Cox, Joint Master of the Blencathra Foxhounds.
Michael Thompson, Joint Master of the Blencathra Foxhounds.
Barry Todhunter, Huntsman.
Kevin Andrews.
Annie Binny.
Duncan Grieve.

The Valley Minkhounds
Aidan and Charlotte Slatter, Master and Secretary of the Valley Minkhounds.
John Newton, Chairman of the Minkhounds' Association.

Hare Coursing
Alan Tyer, Chairman of The Old English and Colonial Lurcher Club.
Elspeth Stott, Cotswold Coursing Club.
Patsey West, Swaffham Coursing Club.
Wayne Drew, Slipper.
Sally Merison, Chairman of the National Coursing Club.
Charles Blanning. Secretary of the National Coursing Club.

The Royal Albert Ratting Club
Peter Beech, Chairman of The Royal Albert Ratting Club.
Brian Oliver.
Kevin Bradley.
Peter Down, landlord of The Royal Albert Hotel.

Rabbiting
Geoff and Pat Fuller, The Three Stags Head.
Paul and Lee Wayman.
Ian Fancourt.
Peter Wood.
Colin Hayward.

The Duke of Beaufort's Hunt
Ian Farquhar, Joint Master of the Duke of Beaufort's Hunt.
Jo Aldridge.
Mike and Viv Hibbard.
Kay Gardner.

Glossary

Account for – to kill the quarry

Autumn hunting – the politically correct name for cub hunting

Autumn stags – larger and older stags culled in the autumn

Beagle – a small scent hound

Blooded – the initiation ritual where a young person's face is daubed with the blood of the quarry after they have witnessed their first kill

Bolted – when a nuisance fox is in its earth, it may be dug out and shot at close range by a licensed terrier man if requested to do so by the farmer or landowner

Brace – a pair of foxes, or hares, more commonly used in the south of England, and in connection with game birds

Break up – when the quarry is dead and is torn apart by the hounds

Breast high – when the quarry's scent is a couple of feet off the ground, and the hounds follow the line through the air

Cap – the hunting day's fee, often placed in a riding or flat cap

Charlie – English slang, as in Charlie fox

Chop – to kill the quarry very quickly, without a prolonged chase

Country – each hunt has a particular piece of land or territory with fixed boundaries that they hunt

Couple – hounds are counted in couples, therefor twelve and a half couple are 25 hounds. The fell packs traditionally do not count their hounds in couples or refer to a brace of foxes

Course – to hunt by sight only

Covert – a small wood or rough pasture maintained for hunting

Cry – the noise the hounds make when they scent the quarry

Cub hunting – young hounds go out with more experienced hounds at the start of the season and learn to hunt. Now not used as politically incorrect

Draw – hounds draw a covert and search for their quarry

Earth – a fox's hole

Field – all those who are hunting and are not hunt staff

Floughs – in hare coursing these are escape holes that allow the hare to slip out of sight, thus ending the course

Foot followers – those members and friends of the hunt who are not mounted. Foot followers can be found running, on motor bikes, pedal bikes or following in their cars

Full cry – when the hounds have found the quarry's scent and are streaming across the countryside following a line

Gay – "John Peel with his coat so gay…". His coat was in fact slate grey, and not hunting pink, scarlet or red as often depicted in paintings. John Woodcock Graves wrote the John Peel song in 1825. Graves was a local mill owner and friend of John Peel. He wrote the song to be sung to the tune of Annie Laurie

Give tongue, give mouth – the hounds bark excitedly when they have the scent of the quarry. Give tongue is more commonly used in the south of England, and give mouth is more often used in the north of England.

Gone away – when the fox or hare has been seen to break cover. A huntsman may blow three sharp staccato notes on his horn to indicate this, and in beagling a follower will shout "gone away"

Gone to ground – when a fox has gone into its earth

Gazehound – greyhounds hunt by sight alone

Harbourer – a person who goes out at dawn to select a suitable stag to hunt

Harriers – slightly taller than beagles, are used when hunting hares on horseback

Hind – a female deer, especially a red deer, over three years old

Holloa – the cry a follower makes when he or she has seen the quarry and needs to alert the huntsman

Horn – the traditional instrument the huntsman carries to direct the hounds and inform the field as to its movement. Also used to end the hunt and call in lost hounds at the end of the day

Huntsman – the person whose job it is to see that the hounds work as a team

Hunt buttons – buttons which are much coveted and awarded to loyal and long time members of a hunt

Hunt servants – professional members of the hunt

Lawn meet – often held on a Saturday when the hunt has been invited to meet before the off in front of a large home

Law – used in hare coursing as in given a start

Lamping – when a powerful lamp is used at night to spotlight a quarry species usually rabbit while out hunting

Left handed, or right handed – in hare coursing when a hare travels in a rough circle going anti clockwise or clockwise

Line – to follow the line or scent of the quarry

Lurcher – a silent hunting dog used for hunting and running down game. Often a cross between a greyhound (sometimes a whippet or saluki) and other breeds.

Lurcherman – person who hunts with a lurcher

Master of the Foxhounds' Association or *MFH* – There are two categories – professional and amateur. It is the master's job to ensure that each hunt day goes according to plan, to liaise with farmers and deal with any problems that might occur

Mask – the fox's face and head often mounted as a trophy

Meet – where the hunt gathers before moving off

Music – the sound of the hounds as they follow the quarry

Nose – the scenting ability of a hound

Opening meet – the first meet of the season, after autumn hunting is over

Pink – often used to describe the red or scarlet traditional hunting jacket. Mr Pink of Jermyn Street originally provided these coats

Puppywalkers – supporters to whom the young hounds are sent and with whom they live for the first months of their lives. They learn their names, basic manners, and not to chase live stock

Rat-catcher – informal hunting dress worn during autumn hunting, usually a tweed hunting jacket and brown or light brown britches, leather boots, a coloured tie or stock

Scent – an elusive thing and a prerequisite for a good day's hunting. It depends on the weather, the direction and speed of the wind, the time of the year, the sex and the condition of the quarry, the terrain, it can lie on the ground, or appear to lie above it – breast high

Scarlet – the colour of a traditional hunting jacket, possibly derived from the colour of cavalry officers' uniforms in Wellington's army during the Peninsular wars. He took a pack of foxhounds with him to the Pyrennees. Foxhunts were schools for cavalry during the Napoleonic wars

Slipper – at hare coursing meets, the official who releases or slips the greyhounds simultaneously from their leash

Speak – the noise the hounds make

when they scent the quarry
Spring stags – smaller and younger stags culled in the spring
Staghounds – now usually large foxhounds
Stirrup cup – the vessel in which a farewell drink, often brandy or wine, is given to followers at the meet
Stock – a type of cravat worn around the neck. It keeps out the wind and the rain, and can be used as a tourniquet or sling. Hunt staff wear an upright pin to hold it in place and hunt subscribers wear their pins horizontally
Tally–ho – I've seen the fox or hare, not often used today. It is a corruption of the medieval French hunting cry 'Il est hault'
Tiger trap – two sets of rails arranged like a pitched roof over a ditch, presenting a clear jump across it
Tod – Scottish slang for fox. Barry Todhunter, the huntsman at the Blencathra, is perfectly named
To give tongue – when the hounds bark excitedly having found the quarry's scent
Trencher fed – a hound that is fed at a farm, rather than as a pack animal in a kennel
Tufter – an experienced staghound whose job it is to tuft the quarry from a covert
View holloa – a long high–pitched scream to denote that the hunted fox has moved away from the covert
VWH – the Vale of White Horse, one of the premier foxhunts
Whipper-in or Whip – an assistant to the huntsman
Wrench – used in hare coursing, when the greyhound forces the hare to make a half turn

Bibliography

A Short History of Crowcombe. Robin Bush. Crowcombe Parish Council 1999

Beagle Club web site

Beagling. J.C.Jeremy Hobson. David and Charles London 1987

Caldbeck. Maureen Allen. Caldbeck Cumbria 2002

Hunting Lays and Hunting Ways. Collected and recollected by Lady Birkett. John Lane The Bodley Head Ltd 1924

Illustrated Guide to Britain. Drive Publications for the AA 1971

On Hunting. Roger Scruton. Yellow Jersey Press London 1998

The Book of Foxhunting. JNP Watson. B.T.Batsford Limited London 1977

The Countryside Alliance web site

The Duke of Beaufort's Hunt web site

The English Season. Godfrey Smith and Homer Sykes. Pavilion Books 1987

The Hunting Gene. Robin Page. Bird's Farm Books 2000

The National Coursing Club web site

The Wild Host. Rupert Isaacson. Cassell and Co London 2001